Poet's
Workshop

Read, Recite, and Write

# CINQUAINS

Listen...
With faint dr...
Like steps ...osts,
The leaves ...p'd, break from the trees
And t...

JoAnn Early Macken

# Poet's Workshop

**Author**
JoAnn Early Macken

**Publishing plan research and development**
Reagan Miller

**Project coordinator**
Kelly Spence

**Editor**
Anastasia Suen

**Proofreader and indexer**
Wendy Scavuzzo

**Design**
Margaret Amy Salter

**Photo research**
Margaret Amy Salter

**Prepress technician**
Margaret Amy Salter

**Print and production coordinator**
Margaret Amy Salter

**Text permissions**
page 12 "House Mouse"; page 20 "The World's Last Magic Bean For Sale by: Jack"
Reprinted by permission of Laura Purdie Salas.

**Photographs and illustrations**
Public domain: page 4 (bottom)
All other images by Shutterstock

JoAnn Early Macken is the author of *Write a Poem Step by Step* (Earlybird Press), five picture books, and 125 nonfiction books for young readers. Her poems appear in several children's magazines and anthologies. JoAnn has taught writing at four Wisconsin colleges. She speaks about poetry and writing to students, teachers, and adult writers at schools, libraries, and conferences. You can visit her website at www.joannmacken.com.

**Library and Archives Canada Cataloguing in Publication**
Macken, JoAnn Early, 1953-, author
    Read, recite, and write cinquains / JoAnn Early Macken.

(Poet's workshop)
Includes index.
Issued in print and electronic formats.
ISBN 978-0-7787-1962-5 (bound).--ISBN 978-0-7787-1966-3 (pbk.).--ISBN 978-1-4271-7600-4 (pdf).--ISBN 978-1-4271-7596-0 (html)

    1. Cinquains--Juvenile literature.  2. Cinquains--Authorship-Juvenile literature. I. Title. II. Title: Cinquains. III. Series: Macken, JoAnn Early, 1953- . Poet's workshop.

PN1525.M334 2015        j808.1        C2014-908192-8
                                      C2014-908193-6

**Library of Congress Cataloging-in-Publication Data**
Macken, JoAnn Early, 1953-
 Read, recite, and write cinquains / JoAnn Early Macken.
        pages cm. -- (Poet's workshop)
 Includes index.
 ISBN 978-0-7787-1962-5 (reinforced library binding : alk. paper) -- ISBN 978-0-7787-1966-3 (pbk. : alk. paper) -- ISBN 978-1-4271-7600-4 (electronic pdf) -- ISBN 978-1-4271-7596-0 (electronic html)
1. Poetry--Authorship--Juvenile literature. 2. Cinquains. I. Title.

PN1059.A9M29 2015
808.1--dc23
                            2014048007

## Crabtree Publishing Company

www.crabtreebooks.com 1-800-387-7650

Printed in Canada/042015/EF20150224

**Published in Canada**
**Crabtree Publishing**
616 Welland Ave.
St. Catharines, Ontario
L2M 5V6

**Published in the United States**
**Crabtree Publishing**
PMB 59051
350 Fifth Avenue, 59th Floor
New York, New York 10118

**Published in the United Kingdom**
**Crabtree Publishing**
Maritime House
Basin Road North, Hove
BN41 1WR

**Published in Australia**
**Crabtree Publishing**
3 Charles Street
Coburg North
VIC 3058

# Contents

# Chapter 1: What Is a Cinquain?

A cinquain (sing-KEYN) is a poem with five lines. Adelaide Crapsey invented this American form with three goals in mind:

- To create the shortest form that could work as a unit and make sense

- To reduce an idea to its simplest terms

- To present the idea in one sharp impression

Adelaide spent years studying poems. She counted their **syllables**. Some people believe she was inspired by a form of Japanese poetry called **haiku**.

At first, her focus was on the number of **stressed**, or emphasized, syllables in each line. Today, most poets focus on the syllable count as a whole.

### Adelaide Crapsey

Adelaide Crapsey was born in 1878 in New York. She attended a boarding school for girls in Wisconsin. Later, she taught at the same school. Her friends called her playful and witty. Adelaide studied in Rome and lived in Paris and London. She returned to the United States to teach, but fell ill. She wrote poems in a nursing home and kept her writing secret from her family. Adelaide died of tuberculosis in 1914. Her poetry was published after her death.

## Prose vs. Drama vs. Poetry

In literature, we use different names to talk about the way words are used. As you can see in the examples below, the same story can be told in many different ways.

### Prose

When the weather cools, watch for the first winter wind. As the sky darkens, snow leaves a light, wintry scent.

### Drama

TIME: early winter
PLACE: outdoors
MARY: Oh, look! Snow!
STAGE DIRECTIONS: [points toward hills]
MARY: I can smell it in the air!

### Poetry

SNOW
Look up...
From **bleakening** hills
Blows down the light, first breath
Of wintry wind. . . look up, and scent
The snow!

—Adelaide Crapsey

We use sentences to tell a story in **prose**. When a story is performed as a play, it is called a **drama**. Can you see the stage directions? They let the actors know when and where things happen.

The third example is a **poem**. A poem uses short **phrases**, or groups of words, to tell a story or share a feeling.

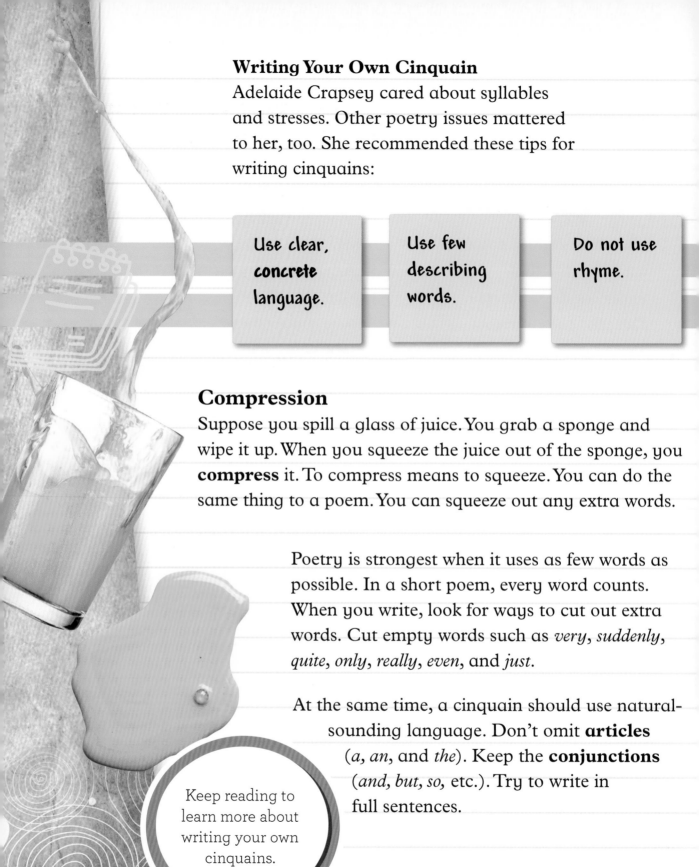

### Writing Your Own Cinquain

Adelaide Crapsey cared about syllables and stresses. Other poetry issues mattered to her, too. She recommended these tips for writing cinquains:

Use clear, concrete language.

Use few describing words.

Do not use rhyme.

## Compression

Suppose you spill a glass of juice. You grab a sponge and wipe it up. When you squeeze the juice out of the sponge, you **compress** it. To compress means to squeeze. You can do the same thing to a poem. You can squeeze out any extra words.

Poetry is strongest when it uses as few words as possible. In a short poem, every word counts. When you write, look for ways to cut out extra words. Cut empty words such as *very, suddenly, quite, only, really, even,* and *just.*

At the same time, a cinquain should use natural-sounding language. Don't omit **articles** (*a, an,* and *the*). Keep the **conjunctions** (*and, but, so,* etc.). Try to write in full sentences.

Keep reading to learn more about writing your own cinquains.

6

## About This Book

In this book, you'll learn about one type of poem: a cinquain.

**Literature Links** explore the tools that all types of literature use.

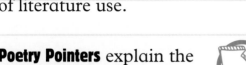

**Poetry Pointers** explain the parts that are special to poetry.

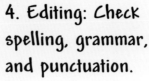

**Thinking Aloud** sections include discussion questions, brainstorming tips, graphic organizers, and examples of students' writing.

**Now It's Your Turn!** gives you tips on how to write your very own cinquain.

## Five Steps to Writing

1. Pre-writing: Brainstorm new ideas. Write every one down, even if it seems as though it might not work.

2. Drafting: Your first copy can be sloppy. You can always fix it later.

3. Revising: Use input from other writers to make your poem better.

4. Editing: Check spelling, grammar, and punctuation.

5. Publishing: Print and distribute your poem, give it as a gift, or publish it online.

# Chapter 2: Writing a Sound Cinquain

Sounds are all around us. What can you hear right now? In this chapter, you will read, recite, and write a cinquain about sound.

In this poem, Adelaide Crapsey noticed the sounds on a frosty night in November:

NOVEMBER NIGHT

Listen...
With faint dry sound,
Like steps of passing ghosts,
The leaves, frost-crisp'd, break from the trees
And fall.

—Adelaide Crapsey

**Poetry Pointer:** Similes
When you write, you could simply describe your subject. To create a clearer image, you can compare it to something else. You can make up a **simile**. A simile is a comparison that uses the words *like* or *as*.

In "NOVEMBER NIGHT," the poet compares the sound of falling leaves to something spooky. She says they sound like the footsteps of ghosts! Have you ever had that creepy feeling? Maybe you shivered in the darkness. Good poetry can give you the shivers, too!

Here are more examples of similes:

as clear as a window

creeps like a lion stalking prey

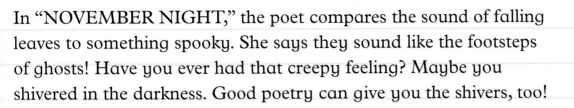

as dark as a moonless night

smells like a rose

**Literature Link:** Conventions
**Conventions** are rules, or the usual way of doing things. They tell you when to add a period or a comma. They remind you to begin a sentence with a capital letter.

"NOVEMBER NIGHT" uses a lot of capital letters! The title is all capitals. These days, that looks as if the writer is shouting. The first word in every line is capitalized. That pattern was common when this poem was written. Now, many poets use a different convention. They capitalize only the main words in titles. Within poems, they capitalize only words that would start a new sentence. Poets can always make their own choices.

When you write, use the format that makes your poem easiest to understand.

9

### Thinking Aloud

In "NOVEMBER NIGHT," falling leaves sound like ghostly footsteps. The students in Caleb's group thought of more sound similes.

"When our dog is hungry, she paws at her dish," Caleb said. "It clangs like a bell."

Kara said, "Sneakers on the gym floor sound like baby birds cheeping."

"Rustling papers sound like tall grass waving in the wind," Sydney said.

"People rushing in the hall are as noisy as a stampede," Faith said.

Drew said, "My dad snores as loud as a foghorn!"

The students listed some of the other sounds they heard.

| In school | At home | Outside |
|---|---|---|
| bells ringing | pets | traffic |
| announcements | alarm clock | sports practice |
| dishes in cafeteria | shower | birds singing |
| clock ticking | refrigerator door | car horns |
| pencil sharpener | opening | waves splashing |
| writing | doorbell | wind |
| papers crumpling | cooking pots and pans | rain |
| backpacks zipping | TV | dog barking |
| doors opening and | music players | basketball bouncing |
| closing | phone ringing | car alarm |
| laughter | singing | ice cream truck |
| calculators, keyboards | mailbox opening | leaves crunching |

## Write Your Own Sound Cinquain

Caleb kept thinking about his dog. He watched her one afternoon after school. He decided to write a cinquain about a sound she makes.

### Sun Seeker

Old dog
circles around
the one spot of sunshine
on the kitchen floor, flops down hard,
and sighs.

**Now It's Your Turn!**

Are you ready to write a cinquain about a sound? Choose a sound from the students' chart, or think of one of your own. Do you need an idea? Stand still for a moment and listen. What do you hear? Pay attention at home. Listen on the way to and from school. Notice what you hear outside. Anything you hear can inspire a sound poem.

If you want, you can include a simile in your poem. It is not required.

# Chapter 3: Writing an Animal Cinquain

Do you have a favorite animal? Maybe you know a lot about a certain bird. Or you might be a fan of dinosaurs. In this chapter, you will read, recite, and write a cinquain about an animal.

**House Mouse**

Silky
whisper-grey mouse
hesitates, sniffs, trembles
surges forward, a quicksilver
river

—Laura Purdie Salas

This poem shows us one moment in the life of a mouse. You can do the same thing in your poem.

**Poetry Pointer:** Turning Points
A cinquain can include a twist in the last line. Have you ever thought of a mouse as a river? The comparison is unexpected.

Try to think of a surprise for your final line. It can be an action or a description.

**Literature Link:** Sentences

A poem should use as few words as possible. Try to omit any words you don't need. But do not cut articles (*a*, *an*, or *the*) in your cinquain. Cinquains use complete sentences. In fact, one sentence can be a whole poem.

To write a complete sentence, be sure to include the following:

 **noun:** A word that names a person, place, or thing

 **verb:** A word that shows action or way of being

That's all! A noun and a verb can be enough for a sentence. Two words are not enough for a cinquain, of course. (In "House Mouse," *mouse* is a noun. *Hesitates*, *sniffs*, *trembles*, and *surges* are verbs.)

Here are more sentence hints:
- Make sure that your **subject** agrees with your verb.
- You can substitute a **pronoun** for a noun.

Consider adding description. You can use a few of these:
- **adjective**: A word that describes a noun or a pronoun
- **adverb**: A word that describes a verb or an adjective

Can you find an adjective in "House Mouse"? Can you find an adverb?

13

**Thinking Aloud**

The students in Faith's group brainstormed a list of animals. Then they thought of actions that animals might do. They listed the actions, too.

## Animals

| | |
|---|---|
| puppy | trout |
| lion | flamingo |
| badger | bear |
| cat | giraffe |
| hedgehog | Triceratops |
| dragonfly | cow |
| ant | squirrel |
| chameleon | whippoorwill |

## Actions

| | |
|---|---|
| stretch | hide |
| yawn | build a nest |
| roar | sleep |
| peep | swim |
| stalk | pounce |
| claw | fly |
| chomp | scamper |
| climb | hop |

If you want to know more about an animal or its actions, do some research. What would you like to know? If you want to find an answer, you can use a KWL Chart.

| What I Know | What I Want to Know | What I Learned |
|---|---|---|
| Badgers hunt mostly at night. | Do badgers hibernate? | Badgers spend 90% of the winter in their dens. |

Start with what you know. Write it in the "What I Know" column. Under "What I Want to Know," ask your question. Then do your research. Add what you found out to "What I Learned." You can use the words in your chart to write your poem.

## Write Your Own Animal Cinquain

Faith wrote a cinquain about a warm blanket.
Her poem includes a surprise animal at the end.

**Keeping Me Company**

Blanket
warms my cold feet,
makes my knees a red striped
mountain hideout for a snuggly
kitten

**Now It's Your Turn!**

What other animals can you name?
Are there more actions you can think
of? Do you need to do some research?
Which animal will you write about?

You can write about your favorite animal, or choose one from
the students' chart. Then check out the actions. Some might
fit the animal you choose. Others might not. Do you want to
create a twist for the last line? Think of an action you wouldn't
expect. Or use a surprising description.

# Chapter 4: Writing a Dream Cinquain

Everyone dreams when they are asleep. What do you dream about? Do your dreams tell you anything? In this chapter, you will read, recite, and write a cinquain about a dream.

Adelaide Crapsey met a friend for a vacation. Later, she wrote this poem about her dream.

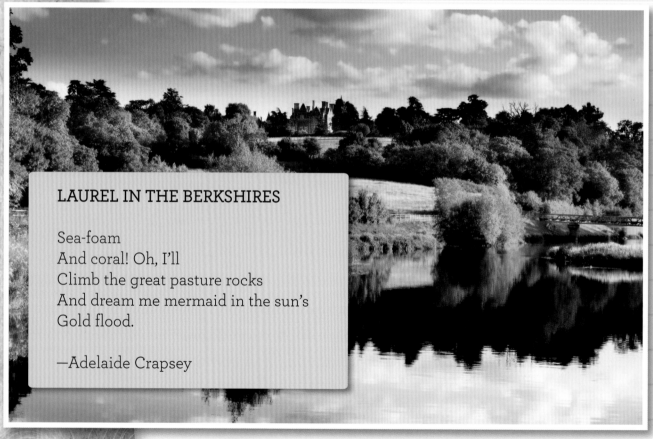

### LAUREL IN THE BERKSHIRES

Sea-foam
And coral! Oh, I'll
Climb the great pasture rocks
And dream me mermaid in the sun's
Gold flood.

—Adelaide Crapsey

**Poetry Pointer:** Metaphors
When you write, don't just describe your subject. To create a clear image, compare it to something else.

A **metaphor** is a comparison that does not use the words *like* or *as*. It can be stronger than a simile because it states that something *is* something else. In "LAUREL IN THE BERKSHIRES," the poet says that sunshine is a gold flood. "The sun's gold flood" is stronger than "sun shining like a flood of gold." A metaphor can use fewer words than a simile. Here are more examples:

| Simile | Metaphor |
|---|---|
| handwriting looks like a chicken's scratching | chicken-scratch handwriting |
| a dog as black as midnight | a midnight-black dog |
| yarn as tangled as a bird's nest | a bird's nest of yarn |

**Literature Link:** Point of View
Who will speak in your poem?
That voice shows the **point of view**.

First person: The speaker in the poem uses *I, me,* or *we*. "LAUREL IN THE BERKSHIRES" uses first person. Your poem can, too. But the "I" in the poem does not really have to be you. You can pretend to be someone or something else.

Second person: The speaker in the poem speaks to someone or something. It can use *you*, either singular or plural.

Third person: The speaker in the poem talks about someone or something. It uses *he, she, it,* or *they*. (That's everyone except *you* and *me*.)

Are you trying to show two different perspectives in your poem? If not, the point of view should stay the same for the whole poem.

## Thinking Aloud

Sydney's group thought about their dreams. They used a **cluster** to brainstorm. They wrote the word "dreams" in the center and circled it. They added ideas about what they dreamed of being. They added more thoughts about what they might do someday, and circled the new words. Then they linked related ideas. Here is their cluster:

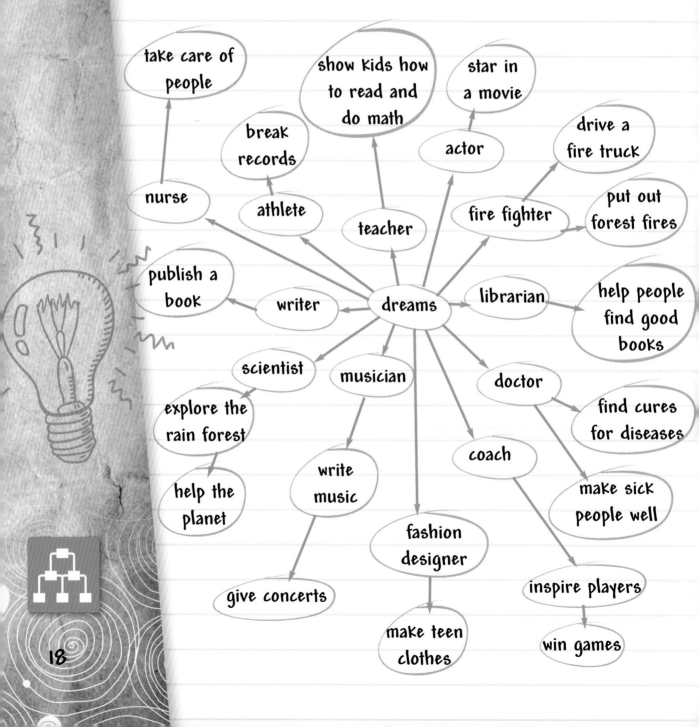

## Write Your Own Dream Cinquain

Adelaide Crapsey's dream is a fantasy. Mermaids and monsters might appear in such a dream. In some dreams, people can fly. They can travel through time and space. Some dreams are like wishes. Whatever we want comes true. Other dreams are nightmares. Sydney's dream is about a goal—a soccer goal!

**I'm a Soccer Star!**

I run,
dodge, slip sideways.
Nobody can catch me!
Past the other team's defenders,
I score!

### Now It's Your Turn!

Think about your dreams. Then choose one to include in your poem. You can write about a wish, a goal, or even a nightmare. Feel free to use the ideas from the students' cluster. You can also create your own cluster to help you think of more ideas of your own.

You can include a metaphor in your poem. You can write in first, second, or third person. What kind of dream will you write about?

19

# Chapter 5: Writing a Story Cinquain

Can you tell a whole story in five short lines? In this chapter, you will read, recite, and write a story cinquain. For your poem, you can make up a story. You can change fact to fiction. You can imagine a new ending to a fairy tale. This poem tells a different version of "Jack and the Beanstalk."

> **The World's Last Magic Bean**
> **For Sale by: Jack**
>
> One bean
> hidden away.
> I want to plant magic,
> but my mother would have a cow.
> Dare you!
>
> —Laura Purdie Salas

**Poetry Pointer:** Titles
The title of a cinquain can act as a sixth line. Think of it as a chance to say one more meaningful thing. Try not to repeat what is in the poem. Instead, consider these methods:

What is your poem about? The title can tell the subject or main point.

Take a word, phrase, or line out of your poem **draft**. Use it as the title instead. Then rearrange the words to fit the form.

**Literature Link:** Story Elements
Story elements include characters,
setting, plot, and theme.

**Characters** are the people, animals, or objects whose actions are described in a story. Jack and his mother are the characters in "The World's Last Magic Bean."

The **setting** includes both the place and the time that a story occurs. In a fairy tale, the setting is often vague. It might be something like "long ago and far away."

The **plot** includes the main events in a story. What is the plot of "The World's Last Magic Bean"?

The **theme** is the main message of a story. It might be described in one word, such as "friendship" or "loyalty." Many fairy tales and **fables** have themes that are meant to teach lessons. To find the theme, read carefully. Think about the meaning of the title and main events. Look closely at the details.

What do you think is the theme of "The World's Last Magic Bean"?

### Thinking Aloud

A fairy tale with changed elements is called a **fractured** fairy tale. The students in Drew's group talked about writing a fractured fairy tale of their own. They made a list of fables and fairy tales.

Hansel and Gretel

Three Billy Goats Gruff

The Grasshopper and the Ant

The Three Little Pigs

The Tortoise and the Hare

The Ugly Duckling

Sleeping Beauty

Cinderella

Rumpelstiltskin

The Gingerbread Man

The Little Mermaid

Rapunzel

Beauty and the Beast

The Elves and the Shoemaker

They listed the story elements. Here is one example:

**Title:** The Grasshopper and the Ant

**Characters:** lazy grasshopper, hardworking ant

**Setting:** fall, outside in a field

**Plot:** A grasshopper plays all summer. An ant stores up food for winter. In winter, the ant has plenty to eat. The grasshopper is hungry.

**Theme:** Be prepared!

The students talked about changing the characters, setting, plot, or theme. You can do the same with another story. Create a new story from an old tale.

## Write Your Own Story Cinquain

Drew gave an old fairy tale a new ending.

**Goldilocks Surprise**

Three bears
left their cottage,
their bowls of hot porridge,
and came back to find another
breakfast.

### Now It's Your Turn!

To write your own story cinquain, you can start from scratch. Make up a brand-new story! Think about characters. Who is the star of your story? Where does the story take place? What problem will the characters face? How will they solve the problem? What is the point of the story?

Try to use full sentences. Give your poem a useful title. Tell your own story in a cinquain!

You can start with a fairy tale or fable. Change one or more story elements to create a new story. You can change the point of view. How would the hare see the race with the tortoise? Think about it!

# Chapter 6: Writing a Rhythmic Cinquain

Adelaide Crapsey wanted the cinquain to have a regular **rhythm**, or pattern. She created a rhythmic plan for the form. When she wrote, she counted syllables and stresses. In this chapter, you will read, recite, and write a rhythmic cinquain.

NIAGARA
Seen on a Night in November

How **frail**
Above the **bulk**
Of crashing water hangs,
**Autumnal**, **evanescent**, **wan**,
The moon.

—Adelaide Crapsey

**Poetry Pointer:** Rhythm and Meter
Like the beat in music, the rhythm of a poem is a regular pattern of sound. Adelaide Crapsey wanted a stress, or emphasis, to fall on every second syllable of a cinquain. She set up this pattern for the form:

| line number | number of stresses | number of syllables |
| --- | --- | --- |
| 1 | 1 | 2 |
| 2 | 2 | 4 |
| 3 | 3 | 6 |
| 4 | 4 | 8 |
| 5 | 1 | 2 |

"NIAGARA" follows this pattern. To find the rhythm, tap or clap along as you read. You should feel the stress on the syllables in CAPITAL LETTERS.

how FRAIL
aBOVE the BULK
of CRASHing WAter HANGS,
auTUMnal, EVanEScent, WAN,
the MOON.

Can you hear the repeating two-syllable rhythm pattern? The stress falls on the second syllable in each pair. That *da DUM da DUM* pattern is common in cinquains and in speech. This is called an **iambic** rhythm. You can see how that pattern started. Now poets mainly count syllables.

**Literature Link:** Alliteration
Notice how the letter *N* repeats in the title, "NIAGARA Seen on a Night in November." Several words in a series begin with the same sound. This is called **alliteration**. Here are more examples:

happy hopping hares

teeny-tiny tiger teeth

purple polka-dotted pants

Alliteration is a pleasant pattern to hear. You can use it in your poem, too!

## Thinking Aloud

The students in Kara's group talked about topics for their poems. They wanted to write with feeling. They listed some subjects they cared about:

| | | |
|---|---|---|
| family | environment | pickles |
| friends | sports | homework |
| pets | music | lunch |
| fairness | equal rights | video games |
| art | hiking | books |

Then they tried to narrow down their topic choices. One way to narrow choices is to be specific. Write about one person, not your whole family. Choose one animal, not a whole species. Here are some examples of general and specific topics:

| General | Specific |
|---|---|
| dog | poodle, yellow lab, Great Dane |
| flower | rose, tulip, lily of the valley, bee balm |
| candy | fudge, red licorice, jelly beans |
| family | little sister, big brother, uncle, cousin |
| planet | Earth, Mars, Venus |
| tree | white pine, blue spruce, oak, elm, willow |
| sports | baseball, soccer, rugby, basketball |

Be specific with your language, too. The more specific you are, the clearer the picture your poem will create.

## Write Your Own Rhythmic Cinquain

Kara is a big fan of spring. Every year, she watches for new growth. She wrote about her favorite season. Here is her first draft:

New Beginnings

At last,
a little bit
of green pokes through the soil.
Tulips! Crocuses! Welcome back!
It's spring!

### Now It's Your Turn!

What matters to you? Choose a topic you care about. You will write with more feeling. Your poem will be stronger. Focus on a specific topic. Narrow it down as much as possible. Feel free to use a topic from the students' list.

Use specific language in the poem and the title. Look for words that fit an iambic rhythm. Use a **thesaurus** to find similar words if you want. Arrange the words in the best order. The rhythm does not have to be perfect. Keep it in mind as you write.

In the next chapter, you can see how Kara's group helped her revise her poem.

# Chapter 7: Revising Your Cinquain

Congratulations! You have just completed the first two steps of writing. You brainstormed new ideas. You used them to write your first draft. Now you are ready for the next two steps: revising and editing. Use this checklist as a guide:

| Yes/No | Cinquain Revision Checklist |
|---|---|
| | Do your syllable counts follow the 2-4-6-8-2 pattern? |
| | Did you include a twist at the end? |
| | Did you use full sentences and natural-sounding language? |
| | Is the rhythm mostly regular? |
| | Does the title work as a sixth line? |

## Group Help

One good way to revise your poem is to share it with a group. Give each person a copy. Ask them to write their comments on it. Ask one person to read your poem aloud. Listen for any places where the reader stumbles. Give the others a chance to speak before you say anything about your work.

Then move to the next writing step. Did they see anything you need to edit? Are there errors in any spelling, grammar, or punctuation?

Take time to think about every comment. Try the ones that make the most sense to you.

The students thought Kara's poem showed her true feelings. Caleb said *little* could be cut because *bit* means something little. Faith said she could move *of green* to line 2. Sydney said she could call the soil *muddy*. Drew studied the rhythm. He thought the title needed work. He suggested adding *Hi* or *Oh* to the start of line 4. Kara decided to change the flowers from plural to singular. Here is her revised poem:

A Fresh New Start

At last,
a bit of green
pokes up through muddy soil.
Oh, tulip! Crocus! Welcome back!
It's spring!

Helping others revise and edit their poems can help you, too. When you read others' work, look for the positive. Point out what parts work well. Be supportive. Writing is not easy. Sharing your work can be even harder! If you don't understand something, ask a question.

# Chapter 8: Performing a Poem

The final step of writing is publishing your work. After you complete the final version of your poem, you can share it with others. You can read your poem aloud to a group. You can perform your own poem!

Practice reading your poem aloud.

Speak slowly.

Speak clearly.

Read with feeling.

You can act out a story cinquain. Choose actors for roles as the characters. Design costumes. Make or find props. You can even design a set for the play. Take turns performing your poems.

Is the story scary? Whisper to hold the audience's attention. Is it exciting? Raise your voice. Speed up or slow down the pace as you speak. Use big gestures. Take large steps. Take a bow at the end!

When others are acting, be a good audience. Listen to the actors. Applaud at the end. Enjoy the show!

30

# Learning More

## Books

*Cinquain Poems* by Lisa M. Bolt Simons. The Child's World (2015)

*The Monarch's Progress: Poems with Wings* by Avis Harley. WordSong (2008)

*Write a Poem Step by Step* by JoAnn Early Macken. Earlybird Press (2012)

*Write Your Own Poetry* by Laura Purdie Salas. Compass Point Books (2008)

## Websites

**Cinquain:**
http://teacher.scholastic.com/writewit/poetry/flash_pie.htm
(Click "play" then click the cactus button.)

**How to Write a Cinquain Poem:**
www.poetry4kids.com/blog/lessons/how-to-write-a-cinquain-poem/

**What's a Cinquain?**
www.eduplace.com/kids/mw/wr/3/wr3_04_9_9.html

# Glossary

Note: Some boldfaced words are defined where they appear in the book.

**autumnal** Of, or occurring in, autumn or fall

**bleakening** Turning cold and miserable, such as weather

**bulk** A large amount or large part of something

**cluster** A brainstorming technique that links related words together

**concrete** Relating to specific, rather than general, people or things

**draft** A version of a poem or story

**evanescent** Quickly fading or disappearing

**fable** A short story that usually has animals as characters and includes a lesson

**fractured** Broken

**frail** Weak

**haiku** A short, three-line poem, usually about nature

**point of view** The speaker's position in relation to a poem or story

**pronoun** A word used in place of a noun; for example, *he*, *she*, *it*

**subject** In a sentence, a noun or pronoun that performs the action of a verb

**syllable** One of the parts into which a word is divided when it is pronounced

**thesaurus** A book with lists of words that have similar meanings

**wan** Pale

# Index